# EASY INDIAN
## CURRIES

S

# CHICKEN TIKKA MASALA

## *MURGH TIKKA MASALA*

SERVES 4  PREPARATION TIME: 15 MINUTES, PLUS AT LEAST 2 HOURS MARINATING TIME  COOKING TIME: 15–20 MINUTES

*Now said to be the world's most popular Indian dish, this actually originated from the kitchens of Bangladeshi chefs in the UK.*

---

500g/1lb 2oz boneless, skinless **chicken breasts**, chopped into bite-sized pieces and marinated for 2 hours in a shop-bought **Tandoori paste**

4 **tomatoes**, chopped

6 tbsp **double cream**

5cm/2in piece **root ginger**, peeled and grated

4 **garlic** cloves, chopped

3 tbsp **vegetable oil**

2 **bay leaves**

2 **onions**, finely chopped

2 **green chillies**, finely chopped

1 tsp **ground cumin**

1 tsp **ground coriander**

½ tsp **paprika**

¼ tsp **turmeric**

¼ tsp **salt**

a pinch **Garam Masala** (*see page 35*)

1 **PLACE** the marinated chicken pieces under a medium grill and cook, turning and brushing with oil at least once, for 10–15 minutes, or until the chicken is cooked through, then set aside.

2 **PUT** the tomatoes, cream, ginger and garlic in a blender and blend until a thick sauce forms, then set aside.

3 **HEAT** the oil in a large saucepan with a tight-fitting lid over a medium heat. Add the bay leaves and onions and fry, stirring constantly, for 6–8 minutes until the onions are golden brown.

4 **ADD** the chillies, cumin, coriander, paprika, turmeric, salt and garam masala and stir for 1 minute, or until you can smell the aroma of the spices. Watch carefully so the mixture does not burn.

5 **TIP** in the chicken pieces and fry, stirring occasionally, 3 minutes. Stir the tomato and cream mixture into the pan, cover, and reduce the heat to low. Simmer 5 minutes until the chicken is heated through.

6 **BRING** 125ml/4fl oz/½ cup water to the boil while the chicken mixture is simmering, then add the boiling water to the chicken and simmer for a further 1 minute, stirring, or until droplets of oil appear on the surface. Serve hot with potatoes of your choice and Plain Basmati Rice (*see page 39*).

# BUTTER CHICKEN *MURGH MAKHANI*

SERVES 4   PREPARATION TIME: 20 MINUTES, PLUS AT LEAST 30 MINUTES
MARINATING TIME   COOKING TIME: 20–25 MINUTES

---

100g/3½oz peeled **plum tomatoes**

4 **garlic** cloves, crushed

2 tbsp **natural yogurt**

2 tbsp **double cream**

½ tsp freshly ground **black pepper**

½ tsp **paprika**

¼ tsp **chilli powder**

a large pinch **ground cinnamon**

4 tbsp **vegetable oil**

500g/1lb 2oz boneless, skinless **chicken breasts**, cut into bite-sized pieces

2 **onions**, finely chopped

¼ tsp **salt**

¼ tsp **ground fenugreek**

15g/½oz **butter**

¼ tsp **Garam Masala** *(see page 35)*

a few **coriander leaves**

1 **TIP** the tomatoes into a blender and blend until smooth, then set aside.

2 **PUT** the garlic, yogurt, cream, black pepper, paprika, chilli powder, cinnamon and 1 tablespoon of the oil in a large bowl and stir well. Add the chicken pieces to this marinade and stir until well coated. Cover the bowl with cling film and refrigerate for at least 30 minutes, or overnight, to let the flavours blend.

3 **HEAT** the remaining 3 tablespoons oil in a large saucepan or wok over a medium heat. Add the onions and fry, stirring occasionally, for 6–8 minutes until golden brown. Add the salt and fenugreek and continue frying for a further 1 minute until you can smell the aroma.

4 **TIP** in the tomatoes and continue stirring for 3 minutes, or until the mixture becomes quite thick.

5 **STIR** in the butter, add the chicken and the marinade and reduce the heat to low. Simmer, uncovered, for 10 minutes, stirring occasionally, or until the chicken is cooked through. Check by cutting a piece of chicken in half – the juices should run clear. Sprinkle over the garam masala and coriander leaves and serve hot with Naans (see page 37).

# CREAMY CHICKEN CURRY

## *KASHMIRI KORMA*

**SERVES 4   PREPARATION TIME: 10 MINUTES
COOKING TIME: 20–25 MINUTES**

Korma *just means a mild curry. Yet, it is actually a very rich stew in which the meat, chicken or vegetables and nuts are braised in cream, yogurt or coconut milk.*

4 tbsp **vegetable oil**

3 **garlic** cloves

2 **onions**, finely chopped

2 **green chillies**, finely chopped

1 tsp **ground cumin**

1 tsp **ground coriander**

½ tsp **turmeric**

¼ tsp **salt**

4 **green cardamom pods**, slightly crushed

2 tsp **tomato purée**

500g/1lb 2oz boneless, skinless **chicken breasts**, cut into bite-sized pieces

250ml/9fl oz/1 cup **coconut milk**

20 **cashew nuts**, ground

5cm/2in piece **root ginger**, peeled and grated

a generous pinch **Garam Masala** (*see page 35*)

1 **HEAT** the oil in a large saucepan or wok over a medium heat and add the garlic, onions and chillies. Cook, stirring frequently, for 6–8 minutes until the onions turn golden brown.

2 **STIR** in the cumin, coriander, turmeric, salt and cardamom pods and fry for 1 minute, then stir in the tomato purée.

3 **ADD** the chicken pieces, reduce the heat to low and fry, stirring, for 7–8 minutes, or until they change colour. Bring 250ml/9fl oz/1 cup water to the boil.

4 **ADD** the water and the coconut milk to the chicken, then add the ground nuts. Simmer, uncovered, stirring occasionally, for 7 minutes, or until the chicken is cooked through.  Check by cutting a piece of chicken in half – the juices should run clear.

5 **STIR** in the ginger and sprinkle over the garam masala. Serve hot.

# CHICKEN JALFREZI *MURGH JALFREZI*

**SERVES 4   PREPARATION TIME: 10 MINUTES
COOKING TIME: 20–25 MINUTES**

*Jalfrezi is a dish in which meat or vegetables are fried in oil and spices to produce a thick, dry gravy. Peppers, onions and fresh green chillies are then added to make a moderately hot curry.*

---

3 tbsp **vegetable oil**

2 **onions**, chopped

4 **garlic** cloves, sliced

2 **green chillies**, chopped

4 tsp **Manju's Quick Curry Paste**
  (*see page 36*)

1 tsp **tomato purée**

¼ tsp **salt**

500g/1lb 2oz boneless, skinless **chicken breasts**, chopped into bite-sized pieces

5cm/2in piece **root ginger**, peeled and grated

2 **green peppers**, seeded and sliced

1 **HEAT** the oil in a large saucepan over a medium heat. Add the onions, garlic and chillies and fry, stirring frequently, for 6–8 minutes until the onions are golden brown.

2 **ADD** the curry paste, tomato purée and salt and stir for 1 minute. Stir in the chicken pieces and continue stirring for 7–8 minutes until they change colour and the spices blend with the chicken.

3 **BRING** 250ml/9fl oz/1 cup water to the boil and pour this into the pan.

4 **STIR** the ginger and green peppers into the pan and then simmer, uncovered, for 5 minutes, stirring occasionally, until the sauce thickens and the chicken is cooked through. Check by cutting a piece of chicken in half – the juices should run clear. Serve hot with Naans (see page 37).

# CHICKEN WITH CARAMELIZED ONION, GARLIC AND GINGER

## *MURGH MASALA*

**SERVES 4   PREPARATION TIME: 10 MINUTES**
**COOKING TIME: 25–30 MINUTES**

*Onions, garlic, ginger, chilli and tomato form the foundation of many curries.*

---

4 **tomatoes**, coarsely chopped

100g/3½oz **butter** or **ghee**

5cm/2in piece **cinnamon stick**

4 **cloves**

2 **onions**, finely chopped

4 **garlic** cloves, chopped

1 tsp **ground cumin**

1 tsp **ground coriander**

¼ tsp **turmeric**

¼ tsp **chilli powder**

¼ tsp **salt**

500g/1lb 2oz boneless, skinless **chicken breasts**, cut into bite-sized pieces

5cm/2in piece **root ginger**, peeled and grated

¼ tsp **Garam Masala** (*see page 35*)

1 **TIP** the tomatoes into a blender and blend until smooth, then set aside.

2 **MELT** the butter or ghee in a saucepan or wok over a medium heat. Add the cinnamon and cloves and fry, stirring, for 30 seconds, or until you can smell the aroma of the spices. Watch carefully so they do not burn.

3 **ADD** the onions and garlic and fry, stirring frequently, for 6–8 minutes until they are golden brown. Add the cumin, coriander, turmeric, chilli powder and salt and stir for 1 minute.

4 **STIR** in the chicken and continue frying, stirring, for 7–8 minutes until the chicken colours. Bring 6½ tablespoons water to the boil while the chicken is cooking.

5 **ADD** the tomatoes, followed by the boiling water, to the chicken and simmer for 10–15 minutes until droplets of oil appear on the surface.

6 **STIR** in the ginger and garam masala and stir in. Serve hot with Cucumber Relish (see page 35) and Chapatis (see page 38).

# HYDERABADI-STYLE LAMB

## *HYDERABADI GOSHT*

**SERVES 4  PREPARATION TIME: 15 MINUTES
COOKING TIME: 1 HOUR 15 MINUTES**

*Hyderabad, the capital city of Andhra Pradesh, has a strong fusion of Islamic culture and southern Indian traditions, which are reflected in its cuisine.*

85g/3oz **butter** or **ghee**

5cm/2in piece **root ginger**, peeled and chopped

2 **onions**, sliced

7 **black peppercorns**

7 **garlic** cloves, chopped

5 **cloves**

4 **green cardamom pods**

3 **dried red chillies**, chopped in half

2 **cinnamon sticks**

500g/1lb 2oz boneless **stewing lamb**, chopped

375ml/13fl oz/1½ cups **natural yogurt**, whisked

16 **cashew nuts**, ground

1 tsp **turmeric**

1 tsp **cornflour**

½ tsp **salt**

1 **MELT** the butter or ghee in a flameproof casserole with a tight-fitting lid over a medium heat. Add the ginger, onions, peppercorns, garlic, cloves, cardamom pods, chillies and cinnamon sticks and fry, stirring frequently, for 5 minutes until the onions start to soften and you can smell the aroma of the spices. Watch carefully so the spices do not burn.

2 **TIP** in the lamb and continue frying, stirring, for 10 minutes, or until it looks brown. Bring 625ml/21½fl oz/2½ cups water to the boil while the lamb is cooking.

3 **POUR** the boiling water into the pan and return to the boil, stirring once or twice. Cover the pan, reduce the heat to low and simmer for 55 minutes–1 hour until the meat is tender.

4 **MIX** the yogurt, cashew nuts, turmeric, cornflour and salt in a bowl. Stir into the lamb mixture and simmer, uncovered, for 3 minutes. Bring 125ml/4fl oz/½ cup water to the boil and stir into the lamb. Simmer for a further 2 minutes, or until droplets of oil appear on the surface. Serve with rice of your choice and Mint and Yogurt Chutney (see page 34).

# ROGAN JOSH *MUTTON MASALEDAAR*

**SERVES 4   PREPARATION TIME: 20 MINUTES**
**COOKING TIME: 1 HOUR**

*From Kashmir in northern India, this is another restaurant favourite that is quite easy to cook at home.*

3 tbsp **vegetable oil**

2.5cm/1in piece **cinnamon stick** or **cassia bark**

3 **green cardamom pods**

2 **bay leaves**

2 **onions**, finely chopped

2 **garlic** cloves, finely chopped

1 tbsp **butter** or **ghee**

¼ tsp **turmeric**

¼ tsp **chilli powder**

½ tsp **ground cumin**

½ tsp **ground coriander**

1 tsp **tomato purée**

500g/1lb 2oz boneless **stewing lamb**, chopped

¼ tsp **salt**

a pinch **Garam Masala** *(see page 35)*

1 tsp freshly squeezed **lemon juice**

1 **HEAT** the oil in a large flameproof casserole over a medium heat. Add the cinnamon or cassia bark, the cardamom pods and bay leaves and fry, stirring, for 30 seconds, or until the spices splutter and you can smell their aroma. Watch them carefully so they do not burn.

2 **ADD** the onions, garlic and butter or ghee and fry, stirring occasionally, for 8–10 minutes until the onions are caramelized.

3 **STIR** in the turmeric, chilli powder, cumin and coriander and stir for about 30 seconds. Stir in the tomato purée.

4 **TIP** in the lamb and fry for 5–7 minutes until it looks brown.

5 **BRING** 375ml/13fl oz/1½ cups water to the boil while the lamb is frying. Pour the boiling water over the lamb. Return to the boil, then cover the pan, reduce the heat and simmer for 40 minutes, or until the meat is tender and droplets of oil appear on the surface.

6 **UNCOVER** the casserole, add the salt and sprinkle over the garam masala, then stir in the lemon juice. Serve hot.

# GOAN PORK MEATBALLS IN SPICY CURRY

## *BOLINHAS DE CARNE*

**MAKES 16   PREPARATION TIME: 15 MINUTES**
**COOKING TIME: 30–35 MINUTES**

---

5cm/2in piece **root ginger**, peeled and chopped

4 **garlic** cloves

2 **green chillies**, roughly chopped

½ tsp freshly ground **black pepper**

2 ½ tbsp freshly squeezed **lemon juice**

½ tsp **salt**

500g/1lb 2oz **minced pork**

2 tbsp **rice flour**

about 5 tbsp **groundnut oil**

3 **tomatoes**, coarsely chopped

1 **onion**, chopped

½ tsp **paprika**

½ tsp **ground cumin**

½ tsp **ground coriander**

¼ tsp **chilli powder**

½ tsp **Garam Masala** (*see page 35*)

1 **PUT** the ginger, garlic, chillies, black pepper, 2 tablespoons of the lemon juice and ¼ teaspoon of the salt in a blender and blend until a thick, paste forms. Transfer the paste to a large bowl, add the pork and mix well. Wet your hands and shape the mixture into 16 meatballs of equal size.

2 **ROLL** the meatballs in the rice flour so they are coated all over.

3 **HEAT** 2 tablespoons of the oil in a large frying pan over a medium-high heat. Add the meatballs and fry for 3 minutes, turning them in the oil until they are light brown. Work in batches, adding extra oil, if necessary. Remove the meatballs, wipe out the pan and set aside.

4 **PUT** the tomatoes in the blender and blend until smooth. Set aside.

5 **HEAT** 3 tablespoons oil in the pan over a medium heat. Add the onion and fry, stirring occasionally, for 6–8 minutes until golden brown. Stir ½ tablespoon lemon juice, the paprika, cumin, coriander, chilli powder and the remaining ¼ teaspoon salt into the onions and fry for 30 seconds, or until you can smell the aroma of the spices. Bring 250ml/9fl oz/1 cup water to the boil while the mixture cooks.

6 **ADD** the tomatoes to the pan and mix well. Add the meatballs and stir in the boiling water. Bring to the boil, then reduce the heat and simmer, uncovered, for 8–10 minutes until the meatballs are cooked. Sprinkle over the garam masala and serve with Plain Basmati Rice (see page 39).

# PORK VINDALOO *VINDALHO DE PORCO*

**SERVES 4   PREPARATION TIME: 15 MINUTES, PLUS AT LEAST
2 HOURS MARINATING TIME   COOKING TIME: 45 MINUTES**

*Goanese cuisine is influenced by the region's large Christian communities
that eat beef and pork, which are taboo in most other parts of the country.*

---

10 **black peppercorns**

6 **cloves**

4 **green cardamom pods**

1 tsp **cumin seeds**

1 tsp **brown mustard seeds**

5cm/2in piece **root ginger**, peeled and chopped

6 **garlic** cloves

1 **onion**, roughly chopped

1 **dried red chilli**, chopped

½ tsp **turmeric**

½ tsp **ground cinnamon**

¼ tsp **chilli powder**

2 tbsp **malt vinegar**

1 tsp **tomato purée**

500g/1lb 2oz boneless **leg of pork**, cut into
bite-sized pieces

3 tbsp **groundnut oil**

1 **HEAT** a dry frying pan over a medium-low heat until you can feel the heat rising. Add the peppercorns, cloves, cardamom pods, cumin and mustard seeds and roast, shaking the pan occasionally, until you can smell the aroma of the spices. Watch carefully so they do not burn. Immediately tip the spices on to a plate and leave to cool completely.

2 **TRANSFER** the spices to a blender along with the ginger, garlic, onion, dried chilli, turmeric, cinnamon, chilli powder, vinegar and tomato purée and blend until a coarse, thick paste forms.

3 **PLACE** the pork in a large, non-metallic bowl, add the paste and use your hands to rub it into the meat. Cover the bowl with cling film and refrigerate for at least 2 hours or overnight. Remove from the fridge about 15 minutes before cooking.

4 **HEAT** the oil in a large saucepan with a tight-fitting lid. Add the pork and fry for 10 minutes, or until all the pieces are light brown. Bring 375ml/13fl oz/1½ cups water to the boil while the pork is cooking.

5 **POUR** the boiling water into the pan and return to the boil. Reduce the heat, cover and simmer for 25–30 minutes until the pork is tender. Serve hot with Plain Basmati Rice (see page 39) and Mango Chutney (see page 34).

# GOAN FISH CURRY *AMBOTIK*

SERVES **4**   PREPARATION TIME: **15** MINUTES
COOKING TIME: **15–20** MINUTES

½ tsp **salt**

450g/1lb skinless **lemon sole** or **hoki** fillets, cut into 6cm/2½in pieces

1 tsp **tamarind pulp**

50g/1¾oz **creamed coconut**, crumbled

2.5cm/1in piece **root ginger**, peeled and chopped

5 **garlic** cloves

1 tsp **sugar**

1 **dried red chilli**, roughly chopped

¼ tsp **chilli powder**

¼ tsp **turmeric**

¼ tsp **ground cumin**

¼ tsp **ground coriander**

¼ tsp freshly ground **black pepper**

¼ tsp **ground cinnamon**

3 tbsp **groundnut oil**

1 **onion**, finely chopped

1 **tomato**, chopped

1 **SPRINKLE** the salt over the fish and set aside.

2 **PUT** the tamarind pulp in a small heatproof bowl, pour over enough boiling water to cover and leave to stand for 10 minutes. Use a wooden spoon to press the pulp and release the seeds and fibres, then strain through a nylon sieve into a bowl, pressing with the back of the spoon to extract as much juice as possible. Discard the pulp and set aside the juice.

3 **TRANSFER** the tamarind juice to a blender. Add the creamed coconut, ginger, garlic, sugar, dried chilli, chilli powder, turmeric, cumin, coriander, black pepper, cinnamon, 1 tablespoon of the oil and 1 tablespoon water and blend until the mixture forms a thick, coarse paste.

4 **HEAT** the remaining 2 tablespoons oil in a large saucepan or wok over a medium heat. Add the onion and fry, stirring constantly, for 6–8 minutes until golden brown. Add the tomato and continue frying, stirring, for 2–3 minutes until it is soft. Bring 310ml/10¾fl oz/1¼ cups water to the boil while the tomato is cooking.

5 **TIP** in the tamarind paste with the boiling water and return to the boil. Reduce the heat and simmer, uncovered, for 2 minutes. Add the fish to the pan and simmer for a further 5–6 minutes, taking care not to break up the pieces, until it is cooked through and the flesh flakes easily. Serve hot.

# SPICED WHITE FISH COOKED IN COCONUT

## *MEEN MOLEE*

**SERVES 4   PREPARATION TIME: 10 MINUTES
COOKING TIME: 15 MINUTES**

*The combination of the coconut and tamarind gives this dish a distinctive sweet-and-sour flavour that is typical of Kerala, in the south of India.*

2 tbsp **tamarind pulp**

1 tsp **ground cumin**

1 tsp **ground coriander**

a pinch **chilli powder**

¼ tsp **turmeric**

¼ tsp **salt**

300g/10½oz **lemon sole** fillets, skinned, trimmed and cut into 7.5cm/3in pieces

2 tbsp **vegetable oil**

4 **garlic** cloves, chopped

55g/1¾oz **creamed coconut**, crumbled

1 **PUT** the tamarind pulp in a small heatproof bowl, pour over enough boiling water to cover and leave to stand for 10 minutes. Use a wooden spoon to press the pulp and release the seeds and fibres, then strain through a nylon sieve into a bowl, pressing with the back of the spoon to extract as much juice as possible. Discard the pulp. Bring 250ml/ 9fl oz/1 cup water to the boil.

2 **SPRINKLE** the turmeric and salt over the fish. Stir the cumin, coriander, chilli powder and boiling water into the tamarind juice, then set aside.

3 **HEAT** the oil in a large frying pan over a medium heat. Add the fish and fry for 3–4 minutes, turning occasionally and taking care not to break up the pieces. Remove the fish from the pan and set aside.

4 **REDUCE** the heat, add the garlic to the oil remaining in the pan and fry, stirring, for 30 seconds, or until golden. Watch so it does not burn.

5 **RETURN** the fish to the pan. Stir in the creamed coconut and 4 tablespoons boiling water. Continue simmering for a further 3–4 minutes until the flavours blend and the fish is cooked through and flakes easily. Serve hot with Plain Basmati Rice (see page 39).

# MALABAR KING PRAWN CURRY

## CHEMMEEN CURRY

**SERVES 4   PREPARATION TIME: 10 MINUTES
COOKING TIME: 15–20 MINUTES**

*Velvety coconut milk and succulent seafood, the signature elements
of Malabar cuisine, combine here in a mouthwatering curry.*

½ tsp **turmeric**

½ tsp **salt**

20 raw **king prawns**, peeled and black veins removed

4 tbsp **groundnut oil**

5cm/2in piece **root ginger**, peeled and grated

8 **shallots**, chopped

6 **garlic** cloves, chopped

2 **green chillies**, chopped

2 **tomatoes**, chopped

a pinch **chilli powder** (optional)

310ml/10¾fl oz/1¼ cups **coconut milk**

8 **curry leaves**

½ tsp **brown mustard seeds**

1 **SPRINKLE** the turmeric and salt over the prawns and set aside.

2 **HEAT** 3 tablespoons of the oil in a large frying pan over a medium heat. Add the ginger, shallots, garlic and green chillies and fry, stirring occasionally, for 6–8 minutes until the shallots are golden brown. Bring 125ml/4fl oz/½ cup water to the boil.

3 **ADD** the tomatoes and chilli powder, if using, and fry for a further 2 minutes. Tip in the prawns and continue stirring for 2 minutes.

4 **POUR** the coconut milk into the pan with the boiling water and simmer for 2 minutes, or just until the prawns turn opaque.

5 **HEAT** the remaining 1 tablespoon oil in a small frying pan over a medium heat. Add the curry leaves and mustard seeds and fry for 30 seconds, or until the seeds splutter. Watch carefully so the leaves and seeds do not burn. Stir them into the prawn curry. Serve hot.

# PRAWNS WITH HOT-AND-SOUR CURRY

## *KOLAMBICHE KAALVAN*

**SERVES 4   PREPARATION TIME: 10 MINUTES**
**COOKING TIME: 5–6 MINUTES**

*A* kaalvan *is a thin gravy-based dish made with meat, poultry or seafood. A traditional recipe from the western state of Maharashtra, it can also be made with fish, such as pomfret or cod.*

2 tbsp **tamarind pulp**

1 tsp **ground cumin**

1 tsp **ground coriander**

1 tsp **rice flour**

½ tsp **chilli powder**

½ tsp **turmeric**

¼ tsp **salt**

400g/14oz raw **king prawns**, peeled and black veins removed

2 tbsp **groundnut oil**

4 **garlic** cloves, slightly crushed

a few **coriander leaves**

1 **PUT** the tamarind pulp in a small heatproof bowl, pour over enough boiling water to cover and leave to stand for 10 minutes. Use a wooden spoon to press the pulp and release the seeds and fibres, then strain through a nylon sieve into a bowl, pressing with the back of the spoon to extract as much juice as possible. Discard the pulp.

2 **ADD** the cumin, ground coriander, rice flour, chilli powder and turmeric to the tamarind juice and stir to make a lumpy paste.

3 **BRING** 375ml/13fl oz/1½ cups water to the boil. Sprinkle the salt over the prawns. Heat the oil in a large wok or frying pan over a medium heat. Add the prawns and garlic and fry, stirring constantly, for 1 minute. Stir in the tamarind paste and continue frying, stirring, for a further 1 minute.

4 **POUR** over the boiling water and simmer for a further 3 minutes, stirring occasionally, or just until the prawns turn opaque and curl. Scatter with coriander leaves and serve.

# CHICKPEA CURRY *CHANNA MASALA*

**SERVES 4   PREPARATION TIME: 15 MINUTES
COOKING TIME: 25 MINUTES**

*This spicy and tangy Punjabi recipe uses brewed tea to darken the gravy.*

1 **tea bag**

6 tbsp **vegetable oil**

2 **bay leaves**

5–6cm/2–2½in piece **cassia bark**
  or **cinnamon stick**

2 **onions**, finely chopped

5cm/2in piece **root ginger**, peeled and chopped

6 **garlic** cloves

1 tsp **ground cumin**

1 tsp **ground coriander**

½ tsp **turmeric**

½ tsp **salt**

¼ tsp **mango powder**

¼ tsp **chilli powder**

¼ tsp **ground pomegranate seeds**

¼ tsp **Garam Masala** (*see page 35*)

2 cans (400g/14oz each) **chickpeas**, drained
  and rinsed

1 **BRING** 500ml/17fl oz/2 cups water to the boil. Put the tea bag in a heatproof bowl, pour over the boiling water and set aside to brew.

2 **HEAT** the oil in a large saucepan over a medium heat. Add the bay leaves and the cassia bark or cinnamon and fry, stirring constantly, for 30 seconds, or until they splutter. Watch carefully, so they do not burn.

3 **ADD** the onions and fry, stirring frequently, for 6–8 minutes until they are golden brown.

4 **PUT** the ginger and garlic in a blender and blend together until a coarse paste forms. Add to the pan with the cumin, coriander, turmeric, salt, mango powder, chilli powder, ground pomegranate seeds and garam masala and continue stirring for 2 minutes.

5 **TIP** in the chickpeas and continue stirring for a further 5 minutes, mashing some of the chickpeas against the side of the pan with a wooden spoon.

6 **DISCARD** the teabag and stir the tea into the pan. Leave the mixture to simmer for 7–8 minutes, stirring occasionally, until it becomes quite thick. Serve with Chapatis (see page 38) and Coriander Chutney (see page 34).

# VEGETABLE DHANSAK *PARSI DHANSAK*

**SERVES 4   PREPARATION TIME: 10 MINUTES
COOKING TIME: 50–55 MINUTES**

*A* dhansak *is a spiced dish of puréed lentils and vegetables cooked in a tangy sauce. This is a Parsi recipe that comes from western India.*

---

100g/3½oz/scant ½ cup **split yellow lentils**

100g/3½oz/scant ½ cup **split dried yellow mung beans**

200g/7oz **floury potatoes**, peeled and quartered

200g/7oz **carrots**, chopped

115g/4oz **butter** or **ghee**

5cm/2in piece **root ginger**, peeled and chopped

4 **garlic** cloves, chopped

3 **green chillies**, chopped

2 **onions**, chopped

1 tbsp **Dhansak Masala** (*see page 36*)

½ tsp **turmeric**

½ tsp **salt**

2 **tomatoes**, finely chopped

1 **BRING** 750ml/26fl oz/3 cups water to the boil over a high heat. Add the lentils and mung beans and return the water to the boil. Partially cover the pan, reduce the heat to low and leave to simmer, stirring occasionally, for 35–40 minutes until the mixture becomes mushy. Watch carefully so the mixture does not burn. Top up with extra boiling water, if necessary.

2 **BRING** another large saucepan of water to the boil over a high heat while the lentils are simmering. Add the potatoes and carrots, return the water to the boil and boil for 20–25 minutes until they are both very tender and the potatoes almost falling apart, then drain well.

3 **POUR** the lentils and any remaining water into a blender. Add the drained potatoes and carrots and blend until the mixture forms a thick purée. Set aside.

4 **MELT** the butter or ghee in a large saucepan over a medium-low heat. Add the ginger, garlic, chillies and onions and fry, stirring occasionally, for 10 minutes, or until the onions are caramelized.

5 **STIR** in the dhansak masala, turmeric and salt, then add the tomatoes and cook for 1 minute, stirring occasionally. Stir in the lentil and vegetable mixture and continue stirring for 2 minutes, then serve.

# PANEER WITH PEAS *MATTAR PANEER*

SERVES 4   PREPARATION TIME: 10 MINUTES
COOKING TIME: 20–25 MINUTES

*This dish is eaten all over northern India, practically on a daily basis.*

3 **tomatoes**, roughly chopped

5 tbsp **vegetable oil**

500g/1lb 2oz **paneer**, cut into bite-sized cubes

2 tsp **cumin seeds**

2.5cm/1in piece **root ginger**, peeled and chopped

6 **garlic** cloves, chopped

2 **onions**, chopped

¼ tsp **turmeric**

¼ tsp **chilli powder**

½ tsp **salt**

250g/9oz/1⅓ cups shelled **peas**, defrosted if frozen

¼ tsp **Garam Masala** (*see page 35*)

3 tbsp **double cream**

a few **coriander leaves**, roughly chopped

1 **TIP** the tomatoes and their juice into a blender and blend until smooth, then set aside.

2 **HEAT** the oil in a wok or saucepan over a medium heat. Add the paneer and fry for about 4 minutes, gently turning occasionally, until the edges are browned. Remove with a slotted spoon and set aside.

3 **ADD** the cumin seeds to the oil remaining in the pan and fry, stirring constantly, for 30 seconds or until the seeds splutter. Watch carefully so they do not burn. Add the ginger, garlic and onions and fry, stirring frequently, for 6–8 minutes until the onions are golden brown, then stir in the turmeric, chilli powder and salt. Bring 310ml/10¾fl oz/1¼ cups water to the boil while the onions are frying.

4 **TIP** the peas into the pan and continue stirring for 2 minutes. Add the blended tomatoes and simmer for a further 3 minutes.

5 **RETURN** the paneer to the pan and add the boiling water. Stir well and leave to simmer, uncovered, for 5 minutes, or until droplets of oil appear on the surface.

6 **SPRINKLE** with the garam masala, swirl in the cream and scatter over the coriander leaves. Serve hot.

# CHUTNEYS AND SPICE MIXTURES

## MANGO CHUTNEY

*AAM KI CHUTNEY*

SERVES **4**
PREPARATION TIME: **10** MINUTES
COOKING TIME: **15** MINUTES

*Chutneys in India tend to be sharp and sour and are served with a main meal or as a side relish for savoury snacks. Although there are countless commercial mango chutneys available, it is rare to find one with noticeable thick chunks of fruit throughout.*

3 tbsp **vegetable oil**

1 large ripe **mango**, peeled and roughly chopped

2.5cm/1in piece **root ginger**, peeled and grated

2 tbsp **sugar**

1 tbsp **malt vinegar**

½ tsp **chilli powder**

½ tsp **salt**

1 **HEAT** the oil in a heavy-based saucepan over a low heat.

2 **ADD** the mango, ginger, sugar, vinegar, chilli powder and salt and cook, stirring occasionally, for 15 minutes, or until the mango is soft.

3 **REMOVE** the pan from the heat and leave the chutney to cool completely.

4 **TRANSFER** the cool chutney to an airtight container and refrigerate for up to 2 weeks.

## MINT AND YOGURT CHUTNEY

*PUDINA RAITA*

SERVES **4**
PREPARATION TIME: **10** MINUTES

2 **green chillies**, roughly chopped

a generous handful **mint leaves**

1 bunch **coriander leaves**, roughly chopped

1 **onion**, roughly chopped

4 tbsp **natural yogurt**

1 tbsp **lemon juice**

½ tsp **salt**

1 **PUT** all of the ingredients in a blender and blend until the mixture forms a thick, coarse paste.

2 **TRANSFER** the chutney to an airtight container and refrigerate for up to 4 days.

### VARIATION

**CORIANDER CHUTNEY –** Put 2 bunches roughly chopped coriander leaves, 2 chopped green chillies, 1 teaspoon lemon juice, 1 teaspoon sugar and ½ teaspoon salt in a blender and blend until a fine paste forms. Add 2 tablespoons water if the mixture seems too dry. Transfer to an airtight container and refrigerate for up to 4 days.

# CUCUMBER RELISH
## *KHEERA RAITA*

SERVES 4
PREPARATION TIME: 5 MINUTES, PLUS CHILLING

*A raita is a yogurt-based condiment usually containing vegetables. Raitas are designed to be cooling, to counteract the effects of any spicy hot dishes. So, if you find a curry too fiery, balance the heat with a milk-based preparation such as this one.*

½ **cucumber**, coarsely grated

300ml/10½fl oz/1¼ cups **natural yogurt**, whisked

¼ tsp **salt**

¼ tsp **ground cumin**

a pinch freshly ground **black pepper**

a pinch **chilli powder**

1 SQUEEZE any excess water from the grated cucumber, using your hands.

2 PLACE the cucumber in a bowl, then stir in the yogurt.

3 STIR in the salt, cumin, black pepper and chilli powder. Cover the bowl with cling film and refrigerate until required. Serve chilled.

# GARAM MASALA
## *GARAM MASALA*

MAKES ABOUT 5 TBSP
PREPARATION TIME: 5 MINUTES
COOKING TIME: 2 MINUTES

*Garam masala quite literally means a mixture of hot spices and is a blend of dry-roasted whole spices from northern India that are ground to a powder. Garam masala is usually added at the end of cooking to finish off a dish with a delicate aroma of roasted spices, but it can also be added with other spices during cooking. Once you've made this, you'll find there is no comparison between a fresh blend you make at home and the shop-bought varieties that have been sitting on a shelf for months.*

4 pieces **cinnamon stick** or **cassia bark**, each 5cm/2in long

12 **bay leaves**

5 **black cardamom pods**

20 **green cardamom pods**

2 tbsp **coriander seeds**

2 tbsp **cumin seeds**

1 tsp **cloves**

1 tsp **black peppercorns**

1 HEAT a dry frying pan over a medium-low heat until you can feel the heat rising. Add the cinnamon stick or cassia bark, bay leaves and black cardamom and roast for 30 seconds, shaking the pan.

2 ADD the remaining spices and continue roasting, shaking the pan, for about a further 1 minute, or until you can

smell the aroma of the spices. Watch carefully so they
do not burn.

3 **REMOVE** the pan from the heat and immediately tip
the spices on to a plate and leave to cool completely.

4 **TRANSFER** the spices to a spice mill and blend until
finely ground. Store the mixture in an airtight container,
away from direct sunlight, for up to 6 months.

## VARIATIONS

**PANCH PHORON –** Heat a dry frying pan over a medium-
low heat. Add 4 dried red chillies, ½ teaspoon *each* brown
mustard seeds, fenugreek seeds, nigella seeds and fennel
seeds and roast, shaking the pan constantly, for about
3 minutes, or until you can smell the aroma. Watch carefully
so the seeds do not burn. Leave to cool completely, then
grind and store as above.

**DHANSAK MASALA –** Heat a dry frying pan over a
medium-low heat. Add a 5cm/2in piece cinnamon stick or
cassia bark, 20 green cardamom pods, 2 teaspoons *each* cumin
and coriander seeds, 1 teaspoon *each* black peppercorns,
brown mustard seeds and fenugreek seeds, 4 bay leaves and
½ teaspoon *each* cloves and turmeric. Roast, shaking the pan
constantly, for about 3 minutes, or until you can smell the
aroma of the spices. Watch carefully so they do not burn.
Leave to cool completely, then grind and store as above.

# MANJU'S QUICK CURRY PASTE
## *MANJU KI JHATPAT MASALA*

MAKES 6½ TBSP
PREPARATION TIME: **5 MINUTES**

*This blend of spices and other ingredients is used to create a flavourful
curry sauce. This paste provides a base to a medium-hot, tangy curry.*

2 tbsp **vegetable oil**
2 tsp **tomato purée**
2 tsp **ground cumin**
2 tsp **ground coriander**
1 tsp **turmeric**
½ tsp **Garam Masala** *(see page 35)*
¼ tsp **chilli powder**
¼ tsp **salt**

1 **MIX** all the ingredients in a small bowl to form a thick,
reddish-brown paste.

2 **USE** at once, or transfer to an airtight container and
refrigerate for up to 9 days.

# BREADS

## NAANS
*NAANS*

MAKES **4**
PREPARATION TIME: **15** MINUTES, PLUS AT LEAST **30** MINUTES
RISING TIME   COOKING TIME: **10–15** MINUTES

Naan, *the Persian word for bread, refers in Indian cookery to this oval flatbread made with white wheat flour and usually leavened with yeast. Milk or yogurt is added for greater volume. Naans are traditionally made in a* tandoor *– a large, charcoal-heated, bowl-shaped oven. The breads are placed on the inside walls of the oven and baked in minutes. Although tandoor-baked naans are more rustic looking and larger than those made in a domestic oven, yours will taste the same. Naans can be cooked the day before, stored in an airtight container and reheated in an oven at 180°C/350°F/Gas 4 for 5 minutes. To prevent them drying out, sprinkle them with a few drops of water and wrap them in foil before reheating.*

1 tsp **dried yeast**

1 tsp **sugar**

200g/7oz/1⅓ cups **plain flour**, plus extra for dusting

½ tsp **baking powder**

¼ tsp **salt**

1 tbsp **vegetable oil**, plus extra for greasing the baking tray

2 tbsp **natural yogurt**

2 tbsp **milk**

1 **PUT** the yeast in a small bowl and stir in 1 tablespoon warm water. Stir in the sugar and leave in a warm place, uncovered, for 5 minutes, or until bubbles appear and the mixture looks a little frothy.

2 **COMBINE** the flour, baking powder and salt in a large bowl. Make a well in the centre. Pour the oil, yogurt and milk into the well, then add the yeast mixture. Mix until a soft dough forms. If the dough is dry and doesn't come together, sprinkle over 1–2 tablespoons water.

3 **KNEAD** the dough by clenching your hand into a fist, then wet your knuckles and press them repeatedly into the dough, pressing against the side of the bowl, until a soft, smooth dough forms. This should take about 10 minutes.

4 **COVER** the bowl with a clean, damp tea towel or cling film and leave the dough in a warm place to rise until it increases in volume and is no longer sticky. This will take at least 30 minutes, but ideally leave for 3–4 hours.

5 **PREHEAT** the oven to 200°C/400°F/Gas 6 and lightly grease a baking tray large enough to hold 4 naans.

6 **PUNCH** down the dough, then divide it into 4 balls of equal size. Lightly flour the work surface and roll each ball into a long oval shape about 0.5cm/¼in thick. Do not roll them too thin, or they will be too crispy.

7 **PUT** the naans on the baking tray, place them in the centre of the oven and bake for 10–12 minutes until they puff up slightly and are golden and flaky. Serve hot.

# CHAPATIS
## *CHAPATIS*

MAKES **6**
PREPARATION TIME: **10 MINUTES**
COOKING TIME: **6–8 MINUTES**

Chapatis, *made fresh every day, are a type of unleavened bread from northern India. The wholewheat dough is rolled into flat circles and then cooked on a hot, flat griddle called a* tava. *In an Indian meal, chapatis are used as a scoop to pick up vegetable and lentil dishes.*

250g/9oz/1⅔ cups **wholewheat flour**, plus extra for dusting
1 tsp **vegetable oil**
**butter** or **ghee**, melted, to serve (optional)

1 SIFT the flour into a large bowl, tipping in the bran left in the sieve. Make a well in the centre. Add the oil to the well, then gradually add 150ml/5½fl oz/⅔ cup warm water. Stir until the mixture forms a soft dough. If the dough is dry and does not come together, add 1–2 tablespoons water.

2 KNEAD the dough by clenching your hand into a fist, then wet your knuckles and press them repeatedly into the dough, pressing against the side of the bowl, until a soft, smooth dough forms. This should take about 10 minutes.

3 DIVIDE the dough into 6 balls of equal size. Dust each chapati with a little flour to prevent it sticking and so the rolling pin can move freely, then roll them out on a lightly floured surface into 15cm/6in circles.

4 HEAT a shallow frying pan over a medium heat until a splash of water sizzles on the surface.

5 PLACE a chapati in the pan and cook for 20 seconds, or until the top surface starts to brown slightly.

6 TURN the chapati over, using tongs, and continue cooking for about 30 seconds until the surface is bubbly.

7 FLIP the chapati over again and, using the back of a tablespoon, press firmly around the edge so it puffs up.

8 REMOVE the chapati from the pan and put it on a clean tea towel. Brush with the melted butter or ghee, if using, then wrap it in the towel to keep warm while you cook the remaining chapatis one at a time. Serve warm.

## *VARIATION*

**ONION AND CHILLI CHAPATIS** – Prepare the Chapatis recipe through step 3, then add 1 small, finely chopped onion, 2 finely chopped green chillies and 1 teaspoon ajowan seeds to the dough. Knead for a further 2 minutes, or until the ingredients are well combined. Follow the Chapatis recipe from step 4 to complete.

# RICE

## PLAIN BASMATI RICE
### BASMATI CHAWAL

SERVES **4**
PREPARATION TIME: **10** MINUTES, PLUS **5** MINUTES STANDING TIME
COOKING TIME: **10–12** MINUTES

*The mild taste of plain basmati rice harmonizes well with the aromatic, spicy and often rich flavours of Indian cuisine. The absorption method of cooking rice, used here, is more streamlined than boiling the rice in a copious amount of water and then draining it. With the absorption method, all the water should be absorbed by the time the rice is tender. After cooking, the grains stay firm and separate and are not sticky.*

*Rice bought from a specialist Asian shop can be soaked for 20–30 minutes before cooking. This allows the grains to absorb water so the heat penetrates more easily and the rice cooks evenly. However, rice bought from a supermarket should be prepared according to the instructions on the packet. Rice can be cooked up to 48 hours in advance but should only be reheated once. It can be reheated over a very low heat in the same pan, covered, with 4 tablespoons water. Or, cover it with foil and place it in a preheated oven at 180°C/350°F/Gas 4 for 10 minutes.*

400g/14oz/2 cups **basmati rice**

½ teaspoon **vegetable oil**

a pinch **salt**

1 **BRING** 750ml/26fl oz/3 cups water to the boil. Put the rice in a sieve and rinse it under cold running water until the water runs clear. This will remove any excess starch.

2 **PUT** the rice in a saucepan, cover with a tight-fitting lid and place over a high heat.

3 **STIR** in the oil, salt and boiling water; return to the boil.

4 **COVER** the pan, reduce the heat to low and leave the rice to simmer for 10–12 minutes. Do not uncover the pan before the rice has cooked for at least 10 minutes. The rice will be tender when all the water is absorbed, holes appear on the surface and some of the grains appear to be pointing up. Test a few grains to make sure the rice is tender. If, at the end of cooking, it is cooked but some of the water remains, drain the rice in a sieve. If the rice is not cooked and all the water has been absorbed, add 4 tablespoons boiling water, cover the pan with the lid and cook for a further 5 minutes.

5 **FLUFF** the rice with a fork, then cover the pan again and leave to stand for 5 minutes. Serve piping hot.

### *VARIATION*
### SWEET RICE

Follow the Plain Basmati Rice recipe through step 4. Put 2 tablespoons milk and 10 saffron strands in a small bowl and leave to infuse for 3–4 minutes. Melt 75g/2¾oz butter or ghee over a medium-high heat in a large saucepan. Add 4 cloves, 4 whole green cardamom pods, 10 coarsely chopped almonds, 10 coarsely chopped pistachio nuts and, if you like, 1 tablespoon sultanas. Stir for 1 minute, then tip in the cooked rice and continue to stir for 2 minutes. Stir in 3 tablespoons sugar, followed by the saffron milk and stir for another minute. Serve hot or cold as a snack or a dessert.

**Easy Indian Curries**
Manju Malhi

This edition first published in the United Kingdom and Ireland in 2012 by
Siena Books, an imprint of Duncan Baird Publishers Ltd
Sixth Floor, Castle House
75–76 Wells Street
London W1T 3QH

Conceived, created and designed by Duncan Baird Publishers

Managing Editor: Grace Cheetham
Editors: Beverly Le Blanc and Nicole Bator
Designers: Luana Gobbo and Saskia Janssen
Studio Photography: William Lingwood
Photography Assistant: Kate Malone
Stylists: Jennifer White (food) and Helen Trent (props)

British Library Cataloguing-in-Publication Data:
A CIP record for this book is available from the British Library

ISBN: 978-1-84899-101-9

10 9 8 7 6 5 4 3 2 1

Typeset in Spectrum and Univers
Colour reproduction by Scanhouse, Malaysia
Printed in China by Imago

**Publisher's note**

While every care has been taken in compiling the recipes for this book,
Duncan Baird Publishers, or any other persons who have been involved in
working on this publication, cannot accept responsibility for any errors or
omissions, inadvertent or not, that may be found in the recipes or text,
nor for any problems that may arise as a result of preparing one of these
recipes. If you are pregnant or breastfeeding or have any special dietary
requirements or medical conditions, it is advisable to consult a medical
professional before following any of the recipes contained in this book.

**Notes on the recipes**

Unless otherwise stated:
• Use fresh herbs and chillies
• Do not mix metric and imperial measurements
• 1 tsp = 5ml
  1 tbsp = 15ml
  1 cup = 250ml